MW01016907

FORGIVES MY SINS

Mary Terese Donze, A.S.C.

LIGUORI
PUBLICATIONS

One Liguori Drive
Liguori, MO 63057-9999
(314) 464-2500

Imprimi Potest:
James Shea, C.SS.R.
Provincial, St. Louis Province
The Redemptorists

Imprimatur:
Monsignor Maurice F. Byrne
Vice Chancellor, Archdiocese of St. Louis

ISBN 0-89243-480-5
Library of Congress Catalog Card Number: 93:77240

Cover design and interior art by Chris Sharp

Contents

A Note to Parents, Grandparents, and Teachers

THE SACRAMENT OF PENANCE (or Reconciliation) is meant to fill our hearts with peace and joy. One way to help this happen for our children is for someone they trust and love—a mother, a father, a grandparent—to introduce them to the sacrament on a one-to-one basis in the familiar surroundings of the home.

This booklet offers just such an introduction. It is written to be read directly to the child. Reading sessions should be short, with sufficient time for the child to ask questions. They should take place in a comfortable and loving setting and at a time when the child will be open to listening.

While this booklet can be used to supplement the formal instruction given in the child's religion class, it might well be shared with the child *before* the school lessons begin. That way the child's mind and heart will already have been prepared to react positively to the more structured lessons of the classroom.

Teachers may also find the book useful as an informal supplement to their religion-book manuals.

Sister Mary Terese Donze

Meeting
With Jesus

THIS BOOKLET IS ABOUT meeting Jesus. You have already met him many times, like the times you talk to him in your heart. But now you are going to meet him in a *sacrament.* A sacrament is Jesus' special way of coming to us and acting in our hearts so he can show his love for us.

In the sacrament we are going to talk about how Jesus forgives us for doing things we knew we shouldn't have done. Maybe you told a lie or were mean to your little brother or sister. Maybe you hit somebody on purpose or took something that didn't belong to you. Even though you knew those

things were the wrong things to do, you went ahead and did them anyway. We call these things *sins*.

Isn't it wonderful that Jesus loves all of us so much that he forgives our sins?

A Big Word

THE SACRAMENT through which Jesus forgives us our sins is called the Sacrament of Penance. Sometimes it is also called the Sacrament of Reconciliation. *Rec-on-cil-i-a-tion* is a big word. It is a good word, too. It means "getting to be friends again."

It is as if you have a friend who has been very good to you, but you do something to hurt the friend. After a while, though, if you truly love your friend, you get over being mad. Then you begin to be sorry for what you did. You remember how your friend was always special to you, and you know you should not have done what you did. You feel sad. You would like to make up and be friends again. But now you are afraid to go to your friend. You are afraid that maybe your friend might be mad and say to you, "You were mean to me. I don't like you anymore."

But then somebody comes to you and says, "Don't be afraid. Your friend isn't mad at you. Your friend loves you and will forgive you." Then, even if you are still a bit afraid, you go to your friend's house and knock on the door. When your friend says, "Come in," you step inside. Your heart is beating fast. You want so much to be friends again.

You look at your friend and say, "I am sorry I acted mean to you. Will you forgive me? I would like to be your friend again." Your friend smiles and says, "Sure. I am so glad you came. Let's talk about this. I am not mad. I always want you to be my friend." If your friend acts like that and both of you are happy again—that is what reconciliation means.

Making Up
With Jesus

NOW, SOMETHING LIKE that happens when you commit a sin and then want to make up with Jesus. Only it is much easier to make up with Jesus. When you are sorry for your sins and come to Jesus, not only does he smile because he is glad you came back, he wants you to feel at home with him again. If Jesus had a house, he would not want you to stand outside and knock and feel afraid. He would want you to run right in and look for him. And then he would welcome you back and put his arms around you and hold you close to him the way people do when they love each other.

Jesus doesn't like the wrong or hurtful *things* you did, but he always likes *you* because he made you. You belong to him. If Jesus didn't like you, would he have died on the cross for you?

Jesus would never say to you, "You are a bad girl" or "You are a bad boy." If you come to him with your sins, he will say, "What you *did* was wrong, but that does not make *you* bad. You can stop doing the wrong or hurtful thing, and you will see right away that you are not bad. It was just what you did that was wrong."

Jesus would talk like that because he understands your heart. He knows it is not easy for you always to be good and kind and honest and pure. And when he sees that you have done something that is hurtful or unkind, he feels sorry that you got yourself all messed up doing things you shouldn't have done. When this happens, Jesus wants you to come to him right away and tell him about it so that he can help you.

Trusting
in Jesus

WHEN YOU WERE BAPTIZED, God put part of his
God-life into you. That means he put something
in you that makes you be like him, just the way
children sometimes look like their mother or
father. But when you sin, it is as if you don't care
about being like God. Don't you sometimes feel
bad about yourself after you have done something
you know is wrong? You feel that way partly
because you feel you have let God down—and
you let yourself down, too.

But no matter how bad you feel about what
you did, don't ever let that make you afraid of
Jesus. That happens to some people. They think
Jesus is waiting in their hearts to scold them.
They try to hide their sins from him. They think
their sins will go away if they don't think about
them.

But it is a mistake to try to hide our sins from
Jesus or to think they will go away by themselves. Anyway, we should never try to hide

anything from Jesus, because he wants to help us when things go wrong in our heart. He is like a good mother who watches over her baby. If the baby gets hurt, she is there at once to help. It is the same with Jesus. When we commit a sin, he is there in our heart waiting to forgive us and make things right again. He feels left out when we try to fix our sins by ourselves. So we should let him take care of us.

Some people stay away from Jesus because they think that maybe their sins are too bad to be forgiven. It is as if they think they have done something so awful that God will say, "Now that is too big a sin. I am not going to forgive such a big sin."

Jesus had a friend named Judas who felt like that. He had played a mean trick on Jesus, and Jesus got killed. Judas thought his sin was too big for Jesus to forgive, and he walked away from Jesus and never came back. The Bible does not tell us, but Jesus must have felt very sad that Judas did not come back and say he was sorry. Jesus would have felt so happy if Judas had come back. And Judas would have felt happy, too!

Peter was another friend of Jesus who did something wrong. He lied about Jesus three times. He said he didn't even know Jesus. But Peter trusted Jesus. He was sorry for what he had done and came back to Jesus. And Jesus not only forgave Peter, he made him the first pope!

Jesus would have been just as nice to Judas if Judas had come back to him, because no sin in the *whole world* is so big or so bad that Jesus does not know how to fix it up again. Never think you have been so bad that Jesus won't ever love you again. Jesus never stops loving you. No matter what you do wrong, Jesus waits for you to come and tell him you are sorry.

But even after we have told Jesus in our hearts that we are sorry, he wants us to go to the priest in the Sacrament of Penance so we can hear with our own ears that our sins are forgiven. It is as if Jesus were to say to us, "Come to me. Do not be afraid. Trust me, and trust my holy Church with its sacrament. Your sins will all be forgiven, and you will be happy again. I want you to be happy."

The Goodness of Jesus

IF YOU HAD LIVED when Jesus walked around in his town, you would know how kind and loving Jesus really is. He never scolded people who had done something wrong and were sorry. He never turned them away or frowned when other people called them names or pointed fingers at them. Once a woman who had done something wrong came to Jesus. She knelt down at his feet and cried. Her tears fell on Jesus' feet, and she wiped the tears away with her long hair. Then she kissed his feet. It was her way of telling Jesus that she loved him and was sorry for her sins. Jesus forgave her. After that, both of them were very happy.

Another person Jesus forgave was a man named Zacchaeus. Zacchaeus had cheated a lot of people out of their money. He was so glad to have his sins forgiven that he promised Jesus he would give the people back their money and stop cheating. Zacchaeus even invited Jesus to his house to eat dinner with him, and they were good friends again. Zacchaeus felt like a new man.

Jesus loves each one of us just as much as he loved the woman who cried about her sins and just as much as he loved Zacchaeus. And to make sure we would understand that he loves us—no matter what—Jesus once told a story about a man who had a hundred sheep. One of the sheep walked away from the other sheep and got lost.

The man left the ninety-nine sheep by themselves and went out to look for the lost sheep. When he found it, he seemed more happy about that one sheep than about the others who hadn't gotten lost. Jesus feels happy, too, when he can save us from being lost in sin.

Jesus told another story about a boy who ran away from home and got into trouble. When the boy came back and told his father he was sorry, his father took him in and was kind to him and even gave him a party. That is the way Jesus is: kind and loving and forgiving.

Sin Means to Choose the Wrong Thing

SIN IS LIKE a big sharp knife that your mother or daddy told you not to play with. If you fool around with it anyway, you can get hurt. Maybe you will get just a little scratch, but maybe you will cut yourself really badly. If you *do* get a bad cut, it will be your own fault for playing with the knife, even though you knew you weren't supposed to. If you stay away from the knife, it can't hurt you.

It is the same with sin. Sin does not just happen. Wrong things don't get inside your heart all by themselves and become sins. Something is a sin when you really *know* it is wrong or hurts someone but you *choose* to do it anyway.

Sometimes things happen that you just can't help. Maybe you fell on the playground and cut your knee. You didn't mean to do it. It was an accident. So it wasn't a sin. Or maybe you spilled paint on the living-room rug while you were making a pretty card for your grandmother's birthday. It really was a mistake for you to paint in the living room. But it wasn't a sin, because you didn't mean to do something wrong. Accidents and mistakes are not sins. You have to *invite* the wrong or hurting thing into your heart for it to be a sin.

Suppose that you are standing by a tree full of green apples. If you don't know the green apples will make you sick, and if there isn't anybody there to tell you that they will, it won't be your fault if you get a stomachache from eating them. You just made a mistake. And a mistake isn't a sin.

But maybe someone who loves you very much is standing by your side and says to you, "Don't eat any of those apples. They look delicious, but they are not the sweet green apples that you think they are. These green apples are not ripe. They will make you sick." But you look at the apples and say to yourself, "They look good to *me*. I'm going to eat one." Then you eat the unripe apple and get sick. You didn't *have* to eat the apple, but you chose to do it. Then the stomachache would be your own fault, wouldn't it?

That is the way it is with sin. Sometimes the

thing that is wrong looks like fun, and you don't listen to what anyone says or to what Jesus tries to tell you in your heart. You choose to do what *you* want to do, and you say no to what *God* wants you to do. Then you commit a sin.

When that happens, you need to go to Jesus and let him lay his gentle, loving hands on your heart and heal it. He will do that for you in the Sacrament of Penance.

Why We Tell Our Sins to the Priest

WHEN YOU TELL JESUS you are sorry for your sins, he forgives your sins right then and there. Then you are free and can start all over again, because Jesus does not count your sins or remember them. Once Jesus forgives your sins, they are gone just like a bubble that bursts is gone.

Some people wonder why we should go to the Sacrament of Penance and tell our sins to the priest if Jesus has already forgiven them. The best reason for telling our sins to the  priest is that Jesus told us to do that. And Jesus told us to do that because he understands how our heart is made. He knows that when we have done something wrong, it seems that all at once we're all alone. It seems that maybe there's nothing good left in us and everybody will stop loving us.

When we feel that way, the only way we can be happy again and feel that we belong is to talk to somebody about what we did. If we try to keep our sins a secret, they will be like a heavy load on our heart. But if we talk to somebody and get our sins outside of us, it will feel like the load falls off and we are free. So we talk to the priest. We tell him our sins. We could talk to somebody else we trust but, except for Jesus, the priest is the only one who can both listen to our sins and forgive them.

Maybe when Jesus told us to go to the priest, he knew some people would be so nervous about their sins and whether they were sorry enough that they would wonder if Jesus really forgave them. But when the priest says the prayer of forgiveness over us, we never have to *wonder* if our sins are forgiven. We *know* they are forgiven. Jesus wants the priest to say this prayer of forgiveness out loud so we can hear the loving words of pardon and know *for sure* that our sins are forgiven—not just maybe.

Ways of Celebrating the Sacrament of Penance

THERE ARE TWO WAYS to celebrate the Sacrament of Penance. Which way you choose to do it is up to you.

Some people like to meet the priest in a special room in the church. They go into the room one at a time and sit down and talk with the priest. They tell him their sins just as if they were talking to a good friend, because Father really *is* your friend. He is there to help you feel at home again with Jesus.

Other people like to celebrate the Sacrament of Penance in the *confessional*. The confessional is like two small rooms with a window between them. We call it a confessional because it is a place we tell or "confess" our sins. The priest sits by the window in one of the little rooms. The person who is telling his or her sins kneels at the window in the other room. Sometimes there is a curtain on the window.

Some people like having a curtain between them and the priest. It helps them keep their

mind on what they are going to say. It's like closing your eyes—you can think better. Some other people are glad for the curtain because they don't want the priest to see who they are. But nobody really has to worry if the priest knows who they are, because Father will never tell anybody anything that he hears in the Sacrament of Penance. He has promised God that he won't.

Getting Our Hearts Ready to Meet Jesus in the Sacrament

BEFORE YOU GO INTO the special room or the confessional to celebrate the Sacrament of Penance, you will want to get your heart ready. Here are some ways you can do this:

- **Pray to the Holy Spirit to help you.** All of us need to be honest about how we say our sins, and the Holy Spirit helps us to be honest. You can say, "Holy Spirit, be with me and help me."

- **Try to remember the sins you did.** You don't have to think until your head aches to remember your sins. Most of the time you will know what you did wrong because something in your heart tells you it was wrong. When you have remembered your sins, talk with Jesus about them. You might want to say to him, "Jesus, I find something not right in me," and then tell him what it is.

After that

- **Tell Jesus you are sorry.** Being sorry is what counts most of all when you come to tell your sins. When you sin, you hurt somebody. If you want to make up, you need to be sorry. You can't just walk away and not care.

Most of all, you will want to be sorry that you have offended Jesus, our God who loves us so much. (To *offend* means to displease or disappoint someone.) Sin disappoints God, who made you to be somebody special and who would like to see you keep on being special.

When you sin, you hurt yourself. It is like you give up something precious because you don't much care. It's like stepping down from being that special person God made you to be. You want to be sorry for hurting yourself.

Sometimes you hurt other people when you sin. Maybe you stole something from them or hit them because they did something to hurt you or told lies to them. You will want to be sorry about hurting other people, too.

And—though it might be hard to understand—you hurt all the people of God when you sin. It is as if you lived on a nice street, and then you let a lot of litter pile up in your front yard. Everybody on the street will feel bad about it because they want the whole street to look pretty and clean.

So for Jesus and for yourself and for everybody that you hurt, you want to be sorry. Here are some things you can do to show you are sorry for the wrong things you did:

- **Think how you are going to make up for what you did wrong.** If you stole something, how can you give it back? If you were mean to somebody, what can you do to be nice to that person?

- **Tell Jesus in your heart that you are sorry.** Most people like to say a prayer that tells God they are sorry. They call it an *Act of Contrition.*

Here is an Act of Contrition you can say to tell Jesus you are sorry:

Dear God—Father, Son, and Holy Spirit—I am sorry I have sinned. I wish I had not sinned, because you love me so much, and it is fair that I should love you, too. I am sorry for all the times I did not do what I knew was the right thing or the loving thing like you wanted me to do. I am sorry, too, for when I hurt somebody else and for

when I hurt the whole people of God.
Jesus, I thank you for forgiving me, and
I ask you to help me not to sin again.
Amen.

We Go
to Meet Jesus
in the Sacrament

NOW YOU ARE READY to go and tell your sins to the priest. Remember, the priest takes Jesus' place to forgive you.

- **Tell Father all the sins you remember.** Say them just the way you would say them to Jesus. If you hit your little brother, say, "I hit my little brother."

You should also say *why* you did what you did. Maybe you hit your little brother because you were mad about something. If you know that, then the next time you get mad, maybe you can wait until the mad feeling goes away so you won't take it out on somebody else and commit a sin by being unloving.

When you have finished telling your sins,

Father will ask you to express your sorrow for them. You can say your Act of Contrition and tell Jesus again that you are sorry. After that, the priest may talk with you for a little while. Listen to what he says. He might tell you to say a prayer. We call this prayer a *penance*. A penance is part of trying to make up for your sins.

- **Say the penance prayer that Father told you to say.** Say this prayer after you leave the place where you talked to the priest. Think of Jesus when you say your penance prayer and thank him for taking away your sins.

If you leave the priest and then remember that you forgot to tell him one of your sins, you don't have to go back again. Jesus sees in your heart. He knows that you meant to say it, and he forgives it just as if you had said it. If you think of it the next time you celebrate the Sacrament of Penance, you can tell the priest about it then. Just tell him that it is something you forgot the last time. But do not let it worry you now.

Before you leave church, ask Jesus' holy mother Mary to help you keep away from sin. She loves you, and she is praying all the time that you will act in kind and loving ways.

Joy! Joy!

EACH TIME WE CELEBRATE the Sacrament of Penance, our sins are forgiven, and Jesus fills our heart with his grace. His grace will make it easier for us always to choose what is kind and loving. The Sacrament of Penance also makes us feel clean inside and free— like a bird let out of a cage. Sometimes we feel so happy that our hearts seem to sing.

Jesus is happy, too. He rejoices with us just like the man who rejoiced when he found his sheep. And all this wonderful joy happens to Jesus and to us because **a sacrament is always something good that Jesus does in our lives.**

The End

MORE BY SISTER MARY TERESE DONZE...

Jesus Comes to Me
Get involved in your child's religious education. Supplement his or her formal preparation for first holy Communion with this booklet designed to encourage family discussion and celebration of this milestone in your child's Catholic faith life. *$2.95*

I Can Pray the Rosary!
In this booklet, each of the mysteries—Joyful, Sorrowful, and Glorious—is simply explained in easy-to-understand language. Sister Donze has illustrated this booklet herself and includes instructions for praying the rosary and a section of prayers. *$2.95*
Bilingual (English/Spanish) edition—I Can Pray the Rosary!/Puedo Rezar el Rosario! *$2.95*

I Can Pray the Mass!
Sister Donze explains the Mass for young Catholics, telling the story of the Last Supper—how Jesus gave us the Eucharist. Prayers and responses of the Mass are highlighted so children can use this book to help them participate in the Sunday celebration. *$2.95*
Bilingual (English/Spanish) edition—I Can Pray the Mass!/Puedo Rezar la Misa! *$2.95*

I Can Pray With the Saints!
Thirteen simple biographies highlight a virtue or quality that made the saint portrayed so special. Each sketch ends with a prayer helping children thank Jesus for giving them such a good role model to follow. *$2.95*
Bilingual (English/Spanish) edition—I Can Pray With the Saints!/Puedo Rezar Con los Saints! *$2.95*

Order from your local bookstore or write to
Liguori Publications
Box 060, Liguori, MO 63057-9999
(Please add $1 for postage and handling for orders under $5; $1.50 for orders over $5.)